I0503589

ART OF THE OPEN HOUSE™

RESIDENTIAL PRO

ART OF THE OPEN HOUSE™

RESIDENTIAL PRO

RJ Salerno

Art of the Open House™

Copyright © 2018 by RJ Salerno.

Art of the Open House is a registered trademark of RJ Salerno International.

All rights reserved. Printed in the United States of America. No part of this book may be used or reproduced in any manner whatsoever without written permission except in the case of brief quotations embodied in critical articles or reviews.

Limit of Liability/Disclaimer of Warranty: While the publisher and author have used their best efforts in preparing this book, they make no representations or warranties concerning the accuracy or completeness of the contents of this book and specifically disclaim any implied warranties of merchantability or fitness for a particular purpose. No warranty may be created or extended by sales representatives or written sales materials. The advice and strategies contained herein may not be suitable for your situation. You should consult with a professional where appropriate. Neither the publisher nor author shall be liable for any loss of profit or any other commercial damages, including but not limited to special, incidental, consequential, or other damages.

This is a book of nonfiction. No names have been changed, no characters invented, no events fabricated. The methods described in this Book are the author's personal thoughts. They are not intended to be a definitive set of instructions for this project. You may discover that there are other methods and materials to accomplish the same result.

For information, contact Genesis Publishing Group at: publishinggenesis@gmail.com

Book and Cover design by RJ Salerno

ART OF THE OPEN HOUSE: Residential Pro
ISBN: 978-1717010735 - April 2018

10 9 8 7 6 5 4 3 2

TABLE OF CONTENTS

PREFACE

THIS BOOK is dedicated to the aspiring Real Estate Agent searching for a pathway to SUCCESS. What will be discussed are real-world ideas and solutions to the ever continued to hunt for the next prospect. These will be ideas mostly not taught in the varying settings of offices where real estate is sold.

According to the NAR 2013 Profile of Home Buyers and Sellers, driving through neighborhoods is one of the top buyer activities, and if the house is open, they will stop on in! The NAR 2013 study also reports that 45 percent of buyers said they used open houses as a source of information in their home search. So don't let the naysayers beat you down and try to convince you that doing an *Open House* is a waste of time. Since 2003, I have made numerous discoveries to help refine the *Art of the Open House*™ into what it is today.

If your real estate career is, in the new phases of life or maybe you have been in the business a little while and need a boost to that sagging career. I have

GOOD NEWS! Today you can change everything in your business of real estate if you dare to believe in what is possible.

I could only hope that the *Art of the Open House*™ will have an impact on you as it did for me. If there is one great takeaway from this book, it would be, "If you think you are a success, a success you will be."

What will be taught truly works for those that have the desire and belief to advance their real estate career from the bottom of the pack to among the top in any real estate office of any country. If you believe, mastering the art of open houses will transform your real estate career. It certainly did for me.

Today you will learn to go from 0 to a 6 figure income within the 1st year of your new career.

To the future SUCCESS may the road in front of you, now have clarity.

INTRODUCTION

MY PASSION for real estate all began when I was about 12 or 13. In those days, I lived in a small but up and coming community during the early 1980s in Southern California. Real estate and homebuilders were going crazy with the amount of growth and demand for more homes. California was beginning to see a rise of a population explosion that fueled the demand for housing. I guess you could say at that time the economy was starting to turn around from the recession of the late '70s and people wanted NEWER, BIGGER homes, the homebuilders were only too happy. I used to go around and see all the new model home communities on my little raggedy 10-speed bike. For fun, I would cruise the communities I lived by to observe the truly impressive sight of so many new homes that were popping up.

It was ON a bright and sunny day in 1984. On that day, they just finished these new model homes sitting atop a hill looking out upon the community I lived within breathtaking views of the countryside, small snippets of an ocean view far out in the distance. The experience of walking through the model home was a unique experience and thought in my mind, how it must be to have a job selling homes. From that day on, I was hooked. Real estate was in my blood. It wouldn't be until many years later, and I would experience the world of real estate.

When my real estate career began in 2002, I, like so many others, approached it with all the excitement and passion, a can-do attitude. Within eight months, I was almost out of business; it was beginning to seem as though my real estate career was flop. Saying I attempted everything to succeed in real estate, would be the understatement of the century. I REALLY, REALLY wanted to make it, to feel that achievement of what I had seen with my very eyes, to feel what those other agents who experienced that sensation of success.

Ask yourself, what would it feel like if you were the real estate agent you wanted to be? Can you visualize seeing your name listed at the top in production of your real estate company, as the real estate broker congratulates you for your efforts?

What is the sensation inside of you as the commission check is placed into your hands?

When saying I attempted everything back in 2002, again, would be an understatement. I almost did not make it in my 1st year in real estate, until one day I would discover what the secrets to a successful *Open House* were. My career was INSTANTLY TRANSFORMED!

As we move forward together in this book, my hope is that you, as the reader may find not only the solutions herein being sought but also find the true power allusively hidden in one's mind. Best wishes to your career endeavors!

Sobering Statistics

Real estate agent success statistics, I believe, are, in general, overlooked industrywide. I know it was for me! Not to be negative on the subject, but some discussion needs to happen while understanding what are some of these unknown numbers to the success and failure of these agents. New real estate agents do not always have excellent guidance early on. People who elect to work as solo agents from the start, for instance, are typically left to figure out what works on their own.

Real estate, in general, has a significant turnover every few years, and the newer agent is usually in the majority of that equation. At times, it might be mentioned at varies real estate training seminars, and one might see it discussed in a real estate article or two, but rarely does anyone speak about the specifics of the "why" when it comes to new agent turnover.

What are some of the causes?

Company-wide real estate brokers are reluctant to talk about the high turn-overs of new agents entering the business, in part when the new agent joins that office they may find the educational resources or training in that office, spread too thin from the start. An agent may overcome some of those education hurdles, or lack thereof, with the right positive thoughts and creative imagination needed, and jump to a real estate office with the right approaches for his or her career.

One would think, wouldn't it be better if the real estate broker had a better plan to help the new agent triumph and do well in his or her new career. Developing newfound sales techniques are important to the business but I feel too much emphasis is placed on that alone. Instead of placing emphasis on just sales techniques alone, the broker could develop more on the positive mind power side of thinking in relation to the agent's business and include those techniques along with the sales techniques with the agent's real estate development. And by doing so the broker might realize greater success by the agent's understanding of how mind power influences his or her new career. Lack of understanding of the conscious mind and how it works, one will continually be dealing with the fallout from losing agents from his or hers real estate office. By placing more emphasis on the development and power of the conscious mind to positive thinking, we begin to understand how that might influence not only the real estate business but also our everyday lives too. Don't get me wrong! Many of these larger companies and real estate franchises have unique training programs to assist in developing a new agent's skills and develop the agent's sales techniques, which could rival the most experienced agent in the business. But none of this matters until one understands the significance of the Mind Science and power responsible for what moves everything.

Unconscious Misunderstanding

Due to my early years of an unconscious misunderstanding of the "Burning Desire" for success, I was unaware of the most critical mechanics behind it. I could not identify those qualities for nearly a decade. As a man think it, so is he. One must assume a person has a reasonable understanding to the mind power within oneself so that when adding to the new agent the phenomenal training programs and superior sales techniques, the complete embodiment of success can NOW take root.

When looking at the statistics in real estate, it is precisely that, a record of who will make it and who will not, but takes no account of what happened. Unless someone analyzes the data and researches what is behind the failure rate, then it's pretty useless. But, for all extensive purposes, one may figure for every ten real estate agents entering the business within six months, half of them will be gone due to lack of money (poor planning) and frustration (lack of vision). As the year comes to an end, maybe 1 or 2 agents from the first ten might achieve trace amounts of success. From the achievement of those couple of agents surpassing the others, one could justify the feelings of early success with an income to match for the reward of accomplishment.

First-year earnings for most new agents with little to no experience entering the industry can be from $0 to $25,000 annually. Furthermore, for every 100 new agents entering the industry, maybe 8 or 9 of the 100 agents will make close to or at 100k net commission for their 1st year.

If you think you are a success, a success you will be. This is the vision and mental mindset one must possess if one is to pursue a career in real estate, or for anything of that matter. A large percentage of new agents leave the industry after just a few short years as a result.

Marketing

Today we are in the wealthiest environment, in history, of technology for real estate. For the younger generation, they may call this the Internet Social Marketing Age for real estate. I have found it to be important to have some working knowledge and a fundamental understanding of marketing. Having some intermediate skills with both, whether it's hands-on or monitoring from a close distance, will save you time and money. For the inexperienced internet user or real estate agent, many internet marketing companies will find you without you trying. Many of these companies range website development to AdWords with google for website rankings. Other companies might have their own specialized - video or audio - services, maybe a deployment of a business Facebook or Instagram page to providing content for your LinkedIn page.

Most internet marketing companies are reputable, but some of these companies may use questionable sales techniques to boost your ego by using words like, "some so-and-so TOP agent referred them to you because you're a top name in the area", or "in the industry, your name had been coming up quite a bit lately." Be cautious when approached by companies with this type of sales tactic. If an internet marketing company must stroke your ego or use scripted words to work your mind's ego, be careful. It may cost you BIG in the end. Personally, my knowledge was more than ample with both the internet and marketing; I had enough skill to design my own website.

If you are like most people when it comes to finances when entering this career, within the 1st month or two, you've just about tapped out funds with all the costs involved in starting your real estate career. It was for me! The thought of spending an additional $500 to $1,500 a month marketing oneself, was almost unimaginable.

Once a new agent realizes the cost associated, with getting a real estate license, it doesn't take very much in spending close to $2,500 or more for some real estate classes, cram preparation classes, state testing, state licensing, fingerprinting, MLS dues, Keycard dues, and REALTOR® Board dues, and you're all about set. RIGHT?

BUT WAIT!

There is more! Don't forget the monthly office dues, the cost for business cards, For Sale signs, and *Open House* signs and much more before you have a seat at your new real estate office. Also, let's not forget that it is recommended that you have a financial cushion of at least 6 to 9 months to keep you sustained while embarking on your new career. One must set aside enough funds when starting a new career in real estate.

I almost became a statistic in my first year, but my unconscious misunderstanding of "Burning Desire" for success is what continued with driving me further. I was unaware of the most critical mechanics behind my success in real estate, the thoughts of my Mind.

When my real estate career began in 2002, I, like so many others, approached it with all the excitement and passion, a can-do attitude. Within eight months, I was almost out of business; it was beginning to appear as though my real estate career was flop. When saying I attempted everything to succeed in real estate, that would be the understatement of the century. I REALLY, REALLY wanted to make it, to feel that achievement of what I had seen with my very eyes, to feel what those other agents who experienced that sensation of success.

So one day a profound game-changing experience would be revealed, and my real estate career would instantly transform.

It was the end of February 2003, and I immediately implemented what I had learned from Kevin. Since then, I have added a few more things to improve it. By the end of that year, I successfully earned a little more than $85,000.

What a game changer to go from $3,315 in the first 9 months to a little more than $85,000 the next. The year after that, I broke over a 6 figure income. Doing something as simple as performing an *Open House* is what made the difference. Some of you may be saying, WHAT! I know.

How is that possible?

As you will find as we follow along together, this has become my secret sauce for real estate success. The *Art of the Open House*, a working guide to walk you through all the steps that helped me succeed and go farther than I thought possible in the Real Estate Industry.

Due to the success, I was having at the time; I had other agents and brokers alike asking me how I was achieving my success. I guess you can say from that point forward that the road to becoming a mentor and trainer was on its way.

Of the people I have had the opportunity of training and mentoring, some have become wildly successful, even more so than myself. It always brings great excitement to hear their story, the impact I might have by assisting the advancement of their knowledge and expanding their direction of success in real estate.

In many instances, when a person is seeking a career in real estate, they need that guided direction when applying the mind power of positivity and real estate technical sales approach to building one's career; with enough time, everything will fall into place.

Fear of Obstacles

When presented with a challenge, do you first think of the ways you could succeed or the ways you could fail? See, high achieving real estate agents are always looking for ways to get to the level of success they envision in their minds.

The issue for most real estate agents is that they invest massive amounts of time gathering information, doing research, assembling all the tools that they'll need for success, and then take little to no action at all.

In most cases, gathering all the tools and taking no action is a reflection of the inner fear that the real estate agent has about their goal.

One of the big obstacles for most agents is that they take one or more steps forward, but because they hit a few roadblocks or have a few issues implementing a strategy, they then become paralyzed by the fear of failing.

When most real estate agents feel that fear, they tend to give in, losing all the momentum they've gained, instead of stopping and reflecting on what's truly going on in their heart and mind.

Most real estate agents never get to the point where they begin to think of dominating a marketplace because they don't understand how to implement winning strategies.

This is where using the marketing strategies learned, and an *Open House*, have been very pivotal in my early success. *Open House* has been the springboard into other real estate activities like home listings. I can walk into any town in the US, unknowing of the local real estate market or its people, and within a little less than a year, be on the leader's board for any real estate company.

There is a GREAT cliché I've heard, and when asking others who have triumph success, many will say it has worked great for them, it's "Fake it till you Make it." No, I am not saying one must go out to their new career and become some imposter or fraud. No! Quite the contrary. All reason and logic may deny the facts of a person's current state of consciousness, but if one believes with all faith, it will harden into fact in this physical world we all see as REALITY.

So surround yourself with positive, motivated, supportive people and don't tell the naysayers your plans. Just do your own thing, follow your dreams, make your own life, forge your way, and show them what success can genuinely look like.

Things to Keep in Mind

- Every thought is a cause and every condition is an effect.

- A person must practice separating oneself from the negative moods and thoughts during all the troubles and disasters of daily life.

- If you can imagine it and you visualize it, you can create it.

- Change your thoughts and you change your destiny.

- Arm yourself with the knowledge and understanding of mind and all other things will happen for one's good.

You are the sum total of your own thoughts. Only you can keep from entertaining negative thoughts and imagery. The way to get rid of darkness is with light; the way to overcome cold is with heat; the way to overcome a negative thought is to substitute for a good thought. Affirm the good and the bad will disappear. Many times most people just need that little direction. Everything else eventually falls into place.

Numbers are Vital

Numbers in any business are vital. Many factors determine success but one very important one is numbers. Hosting an *Open House* is in some ways no different from the person running a Hot Dog stand on a street corner. He needs product, people and sales to be in business and if there is a problem with the product, he changes it. If the traffic of people coming to his stand is low, he shifts location to attract more people. More people = more opportunity for potential sales. That's all; *Open House* is the potential for an opportunity.

As I stress, numbers are the key. Opportunity for success is far greater for the person that says, hosts eight open houses as opposed to the person that only hosts one for the month. Opportunity can vary. In the past, I have hosted *Open House* only to have no one show for the day. Other times I had an astounding turnout with 46+ people to the *Open House*.

One of the many successful open houses experienced, was when once I had a woman come to an *Open House* on a Thursday afternoon. In the conversation, I found out that she had just fired her real estate agent. On that day, the opportunity led to 4 home sales and closed in less than 45 days.

Another occasion I had an *Open House*, was on Super Bowl Sunday. The agents in the office thought I was crazy, and maybe so, but I ensured the *Open House* would have plenty of big screen TVs for that day.

Sometimes, it's not the *Open House* you sell, but the one a couple of houses over.

Now it was Super Bowl Sunday, and the turnout was poor. No one had shown and at about 4:30 in the afternoon, I was preparing to close down when all of a sudden, there came a knock on the door. It was a couple hoping to see the home. As I later learned, they were in town from another state for the weekend. I did not sell the *Open House* that day, but instead put under contract and sold to them another home the next block over. That home was listed for $775,000.

To have a mindset right, one must understand there might be open houses where possibly no one shows, or turnout is light. It will be the consistency of how many open houses are done for the week or month that will build on your opportunity of meeting new prospects. If the turnout is less than desirable twice at an *Open House*, I may choose another home in hopes to increase turnout. This goes back to choosing the right home for your *Open House*.

Once, I chose a beautiful home for an *Open House*, the turnout was poor for the Saturday and Sunday I had open. The next week, I attempted a Thursday *Open House* with what would end up to be another poor turnout.

Disappointed with the turnout, I was preparing to close down the *Open House* and then, without notice, a car pulled into the driveway. As viewed out the kitchen window, a man was approaching the home and walking up the driveway from his car. He looked as though he was coming home from work and made a detour to my *Open House* as he was still wearing his work clothes. He came into the home, and I introduced myself to him. I won't forget that one of his questions to me was, "Who does an *Open House* on a Thursday?" To which I quickly responded, "I do, after all, it brought you in today, RIGHT?" as I chuckled.

In the midst of closing down the *Open House*, the man asked quickly if he could call his wife for her to come over and see the home. After all, they lived two street blocks over, and I responded, "Sure no problem!"

What was originally thought to be a poor turnout, became a sale and a listing that Thursday afternoon. The man and his wife, who came over later, would be the ones to buy the *Open House* and allow me to list their home For Sale just two street blocks over. When least expected opportunity will present itself.

In many instances, when a person is seeking a career in real estate, they need that concise direction when applying the mind power of positivity and real estate technical sales approach to building one's career; with enough time, everything will fall into place.

Numbers in any business are vital. A real estate business is no different. Many factors determine success, but one essential aspect is the vision needed and imagination required to see success when the objective world around you denies the very reality of it.

The numbers within a real estate office from the higher-ups are seldom spoken about unless it's the office broker or manager working to grow their agent population. Not to say there is anything wrong with that, but to the new real estate agent interviewing varies real estate offices, one needs to find the right fit and not cave into just the company name. While some real estate offices have a keen sense of not only growing their office, they also put resources into retaining their top agents. Other real estate offices put a considerable amount of resources into new agent development and training specifically. As a new real estate agent, one must have a plan in effect for that type of real estate office suited to that person's personality and focus on what will work best for you.

When searching where to hang your real estate license, there is no right or wrong real estate office to work for. The agent who is deciding on a real estate office will need to find clarity with any internal office prospect policies and training programs available. One ultimate question in every new agent's mind should be, what is being taught relevant, and if applied, can it help me in my new career? Selecting the right real estate office can make or break a new agent who ultimately is seeking a pathway to success.

I began to teach classes on my success on *Open House*.

Of all the real estate offices I have worked for since getting my real estate license in 2002, none of them had a training program on how *Open House* could work for the agent, let alone the great prospecting possibilities. Usually, it wasn't too long after arriving that I would be asked by the office broker or manager if I would teach my *Open House* classes or mentor fellow agents on how I was doing it. I was always happy to do so!

After moving to Texas, I would again figure out that the techniques to *Open House* would be relevant for today's market when getting my real estate license in 2012. Just like 10 years earlier, I came to a new city where I had no contacts or sphere of influence and had to start from the ground up.

With 15 months' time, I would have the opportunity to rank by production among the TOP 21 agents out of 240 agents for the #1 ranked big name office in 2013.

All my success attributed to the techniques of the *Art of the Open House*™.

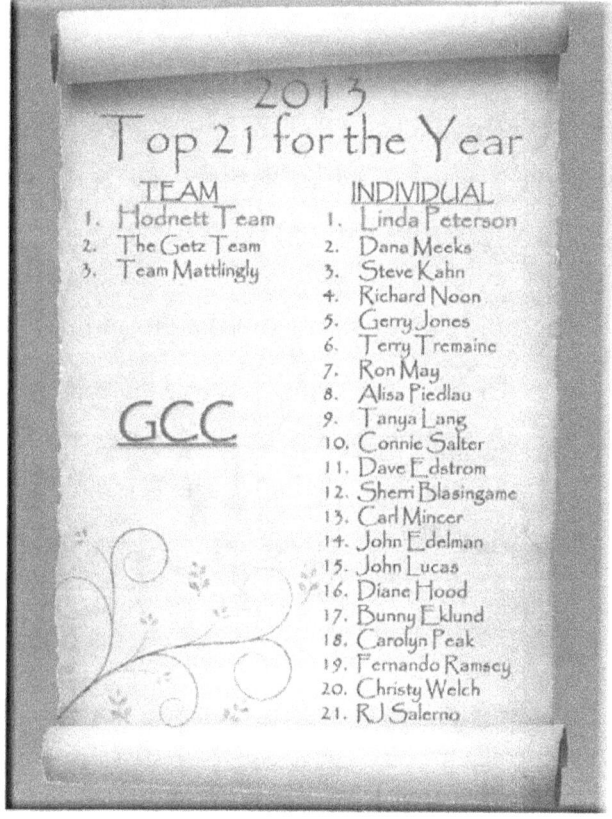

In my 1ST year, I ranked among the TOP 21 out of 240 agents for 2013.

Home Buyers & Sellers

In general, real estate agents chasing after potential leads have become something of a cliché. What very few mention, there is an art to it. It all begins with relationship building.

Relationships are your bread and butter—and when I say that, I'm not talking about the little dinner rolls you fill up on before your meal arrives.

To understand how to maximize your relationships as a real estate agent, start by asking the fundamental questions: whom do you know, and who knows you? Knowing and being known by as many people as possible is crucial, especially when there aren't a lot of prospects to go around.

I have found the platform of an *Open House* to be a great tool of opportunity. It all begins with the first impression, which leads to kindling that relationship. When successfully conducting many open houses throughout the months and years to come, you will find people who come to an *Open House* of yours and remember you from a prior one they visited.

According to the NAR 2013 Profile of Home Buyers and Sellers, driving through neighborhoods is one of the top buyer activities, and if the house is open, they will stop on in!

Not to deter anyone from the negative, "NO's" one may receive from a potential prospect, but it is important to note, one must enjoy, or learn to enjoy, in bathing in the word, "NO." It will be heard more times than the, "YES" that all real estate agents desire to hear. Don't worry, in time you'll build up your immunity to it. Sometimes it's just the prospect saying to you they have not heard enough to give that approval of a, "Yes." Each prospecting method has positives and negatives to it, and that is really up to the real estate agent.

I found *Open House* to be a more convenient method since it gave a more casual way to introduce myself to a prospective buyer or seller. Whereas other methods could be more abrasive or costly to the new agent when starting in his or her young career. I believe on the list of least favorite, would have to be, "Cold Calling". I don't think we need to go into detail on that.

Farming is another possibility if one is not in a rush to generate money immediately. Usual expected R.O.I. is typically one to three years before seeing the fruits and labor of farming if done right. However, in today's mobile and Internet world, agents must adapt to achieve any success when farming neighborhoods. Whatever way, time will always play a crucial factor.

In my career, I have found that offering advice to people who are not seeking information, to be less than fruitful. Those who want information will seek you out, so spend your time wisely.

On the subject of sphere of influence, I do want to touch on this prospecting method. It seems that most real estate sales managers suggest to, just about, any new real estate associates to, "reach out to your sphere of influence." Reaching out to a sphere of influence may work for some, but ask yourself, who really wants to be on the receiving end of a friend, relative, or past coworker, hustling for real estate proposes? For some this may not be a viable approach to grow one's database of contacts. Personally, for me, this approach did not work in my business model of real estate.

The untold truth is, most people, if given a choice, would not want to work with a rookie, even if that rookie is a friend or family. Get some experience under your belt, "Would be the words spoken," and maybe we'll talk.

Out of all the prospecting methods, I believe *Open House* to be the least costly in funds with the most immediate results approach out of them all. It's not to say the other prospecting methods don't work, but a good majority of them require more time to develop and more money, which most new agents lack to see the fruits of the labor.

- Cold calling.

- Offering home appraisal door-to-door.

- Offer advice to FSBOs.

- Farming neighborhoods.

- Calling expired real estate listings.

- Facebook, Twitter, & Zillow advertising etc.

- Send Just Listed & Sold E-Cards / e-Flyers.

- Send holiday cards & mailers.

- Reconnect with past clients, family & friends.

- *OPEN HOUSE* and Many more…

If you're having a problem getting people to hire you as their real estate agent, it's probably because they don't know why they should choose you over any other agent. However, more disturbing than the fact that the prospects don't know why they should choose you over any other real estate agent, is the fact that most agents don't even know why the prospect should choose them either.

Therefore, the first question you must answer in your own mind is,

"Why should a prospect choose me over any and every other option for buying or selling a house that's available to them, including doing nothing?"

Once you have identified that crucial marketing point for yourself, now you're ready to stand out from the other agents, who put very little importance to this valuable detail of Identity Marketing.

Stop Selling the Open House

Even through all the changes technology has made in how homes are bought and sold, one standard feature of the process remains the *Open House*. Technology may make it easier, but it can never replace the human connection of experience.

However, has the *Open House* gone the way of the landline and outlived its usefulness? It depends on whom you ask. Some agents believe modern life has rendered open houses unnecessary, while other agents believe they are more critical than ever. I think when artificial intelligence becomes the factor in replacing humanity, only then will be the day when an *Open House* is rendered useless. Stop being a real estate salesperson and become a real estate marketer. Salespeople sell clients what they have. Marketers make sure they have what clients want to buy.

While some agents believe *Open House* maybe be a vital tool to sell the *Open House*, this is where opportunity is missed. They have the wrong mindset when hosting an *Open House*. It's not about selling, yet some agents continue to miss this premise and ponder why they aren't succeeding. Yes, it would be nice to sell the *Open House*, but when a prospect feels they are being sold or a home is being pushed on them, in most cases, they RUN.

An *Open House* is a tool for the seller, which can give exposure to a seller's home. Whether by street signs, newspaper ads, or internet ads that are promoting the *Open House*, having an *Open House* can lead to exposure and not just for the seller but also for real estate agent hosting the Open House.

If the agent continues with that mindset of attempting to sell the *Open House*, eventually, the agent will give up on the belief of conducting open houses, and condemn open houses as that valuable tool of opportunity. That is where most negative feedback from other agents is expressed, why they don't believe *Open House* to be an opportunity. One of the biggest marketing mistakes real estate agents make is not understanding and addressing potential client needs.

It's NOT about selling the *Open House*; it's about meeting people who might be thinking of buying or selling shortly.

Important to note, a surprising 16% of the time, the real estate agent does end up SELLING the

Open House. The mindset must be RIGHT when approaching the reason to host the *Open House*!

Committing to the *Art of the Open House*™ certainly opens the possibilities in meeting 3 to 6 new prospects on average for each *Open House*. Also, don't forget the possibility of meeting someone who might be considering to sell their home, too. If done right, an *Open House* can be a very SUCCESSFUL tool.

If you're looking for greater success in the *Open House* arena, the first thing you need to know is how to get prospective buyers to show up. One of the best ways to attract people is by promoting the *Open House* as widely as you can and as early as possible in the place where most buyers are lurking—on the Internet.

The marketing strategy is the usage of signs, and lots of them. Use a mix of company-branded signs and specialty signs, which advertise giveaways ranging from fresh-brewed coffee to a list of area foreclosures.

Psychology of Open House

Understand most prospects will be reluctant to talk to you in the beginning. It's much the same if you have ever gone to a car lot browsing for your next new car. Have you ever walked onto a car lot and announced that you're here to buy a car?

NO OF COURSE NOT!

If you're like many, you may have already given your last rights, prepared a eulogy for that old car of yours and parked out of sight from any potential car salespeople to see.

WHY?

You don't want that salesperson to know why you're there. The phrase, "I'm just looking" comes up a lot. Why? You haven't decided if that person can really relate to you, your needs and wants. A relationship hasn't been established.

The public's view of real estate agents is maybe a notch above a car salesperson AND the car salesperson is most likely around the bottom rung to the public's eye, or so I have heard. So, for all those car salespeople out there, you can put down your pitchforks, but maybe it's time for a career change to real estate.

As I would say, you have, "5.9 seconds," to make an impression and to begin kindling a relationship that can have great return years.

If that prospect is already not working with a real estate agent, this is truly the moment when you need to shine the most. This has the potential of defining the phrase, "Your Real Estate Agent for Life."

From the moment buyers walk through the door, they will be grading your first five to ten words, as well as what your body language says to them. If a connection is made, this will be the water so your fruit can grow.

Keep in perspective that since you are hosting an *Open House*, it is mindful to remember that people are coming to you, not the other way around. You are not the one showing up at a person's home, unannounced, to talk to them about real estate. For 3 or 4 hours, that *Open House* is your home, to do what with? To talk about real estate, of course! This is the moment when the confidence inside yourself and your ability must shine the brightest. This may be the only time you'll see your house guests again. Being the resident neighborhood PRO and area specialist is the overlapping goal.

We could be the problem, or the solution to the problem, the mindset is what makes the difference.

TIME TO GET BUSY

They must see you as the PROFESSIONAL, and not just some salesperson trying to make a buck. This is an area believed to be easily overlooked. Most home buyers and sellers prefer to work with someone that connects with them, understands their wants and needs, and that is where the dilemma appears.

We, as professionals, are told from day one coming into this industry that it's all business, and to conduct it professionally. For the buyer or seller, it's about the business of their home, or soon-to-be-home, but for both buyer and seller, there is a very present emotional connection to the whole process. This decision made upon them will likely be the BIGGEST lifestyle event experienced by the buyer or seller.

Do you see now why the connection part plays a huge role? If the agent gets that part right with success, this will set in motion a refer base that will multiply for years to come.

To be ready, the agent needs planning, preparation, and discipline. Remember in the beginning, that it's important to keep the conversation light and airy. If the prospect sees you relaxed, they will eventually open up.

Know that from the moment the prospect enters the *Open House*; their guard is up. Can you blame them? Society has told them that real estate agents have fangs and are scarier than Freddy Krueger.

If an agent is trying to decide where the best place is to set up command central. Let me suggest the kitchen. Please don't be that agent, the one that sets up a card table and chair right next to the front door as your visitors enter through. They might get a good scare and start to believe in society's rumors of them. Give your prospect some space, then meet and greet them. Get them to smile, laugh, and begin with some easy icebreakers questions.

Here are some icebreaker questions that may help.

- What brought them in?

- What prompted you to look into (purchasing / selling) a home?

- What is their ideal home?

- What is their ideal area?

- What price range has been established for this?

- What are they involved in… (Their job / the community / hobbies)?

Once past the meet and greet, this is where understanding body language is important. As a real estate professional, you should always be mindful of your body language. It influences the first impression you make on others and can attract or repel potential prospects. Do you fidget when you're talking to your prospective clients? Where are your hands? How is your posture? Are you authentic and welcoming? If you're confident, you will not only impress those you're talking to, but you'll have more self-confidence as well.

When you walk into a room, be confident in your movements. Don't cross your arms or hunch your shoulders. When sitting, practice an expansive body language - take up as much space as possible without invading your prospect's personal space to appear powerful and assertive.

The prospect may want to roam through the home first, and talk later. They may want to be guided through the home and talk as they look around.

Open-ended questions are incredibly valuable to the home sales process (as long as you listen).

They help you gather information, qualify opportunities, and establish rapport, trust, and credibility.

As a real estate professional, it's very important to have a repertoire of powerful open-ended questions. Questions that are answered by more than a simple "yes" or "no." Questions where the prospect/client gets directly involved in the sales discussion. Here are some examples.

- What do they see as the next action steps?

- When are they planning to make it happen?

- What kind of challenges they are facing?

- What are their concerns?

- How do they see this happening?

- What are their expectations / requirements for a smooth real estate transaction?

- What is the timeline for the process?

- What would they most like to see accomplished?

The whole point of using open-ended questions in a sales dialogue is to invite the prospect to open up, elaborate on key points, and be forthcoming with new and meaningful information. Sometimes starting with, "Tell me about…", can achieve the same end, even though it's not technically a question.

As a real estate agent, it's important to let clients know you are someone they can trust. Be the one who is different … a standout from the rest!

Open-end questions for... the …. **WIN!**

Buyer Dropped the "A" Bomb

What phrase is the quickest way to get rid of a real estate agent? Simple! By the potential prospect saying, I'm WORKING with another real estate "**AGENT**." BOOM, as the agent hears the devastating words for the prospect's mouth! Apparently, that phrase, I'm WORKING with another real estate "**AGENT**" is kryptonite for many real estate agents, which most agents don't recover from in the initial meet and greet with their prospect.

It's not to say the potential prospect is lying, it just they don't know you. There is no relationship established yet with you. The potential prospect may be working with another real estate agent, but is that a valid reason for the *Open House* agent to not engage in conversion him / her? NO! Of course, not, it's perfectly fine. You just can't steal the other agent's client, "if" there is a working relationship between the both of them.

Many times, I heard that phase when in reality they were just shopping for a real estate agent or thinking of replacing their current one, and that agent stood right before the prospect wasn't clued on the signs the prospect was giving off. They missed their opportunity. Remember, stop being a real estate salesperson and become a real estate marketer. Salespeople sell clients what they have. Real Estate Marketers make sure they have what clients want to buy.

In some states, a buyer might sign a buyer's representation agreement with their current agent's broker, but that doesn't prohibit you from interacting with the prospect, so long as you don't mislead them.

For clarity, a Buyer Representation Agreement, is a legal document that creates a working relationship with a particular buyer's real estate agent/broker, detailing what services the client is entitled to and what a buyer's real estate agent expects from the buyer in return. No agent has the claim on a buyer, and the buyer can switch to another real estate agent if they prefer to.

By all means, I am not suggesting that you convince a prospective client to switch agents, or tell them to fire their current real estate agent. That would be unethical. What I am suggesting is to be aware of the opportunities if they present themselves, then capitalize on them. Always get clarification from your real estate broker as to his or her policies regarding Buyer Representation.

Below is a short list of why a prospect might be considering changing real estate agents.

- Poor communication skills.
- Cannot adequately answer questions.

- Seems unfamiliar with the neighborhood.

- Shows homes that do not fit the parameters.

- Does not respond promptly to inquiries.

- Appears more interested in his/her own needs than the client.

- Gets easily confused or distracted from job at hand.

- Personal style is not a good match for client personality.

- Lacks a visible quality that is important to client.

- Shows evidence of a weak negotiation ability.

Be alert; you might miss that the prospect is shopping for a new real estate agent. It happens.

Here are some of the ways that a Home Buyer or Seller may want to measure searching for the right real estate agent to work with, they may want to:

- Talk with recent clients of theirs.

- Check for license and disciplinary actions.

- Ask about professional awards.

- Select an agent with the right credentials.

- Find out how experienced an agent is.

- Look at the agent's current listings.

- Gauge the agent's knowledge of the area.

Searching for the right home to have an *Open House* is vital.

Educated Homebuyer

Today's home buyers and sellers are more educated consumers, due to the many internet resources available to them. Over the last 20 years, the way technology has influenced our lives is very evident in every walk of life. The Real Estate industry has become faster, easier, and more reliable in the last twenty years, thanks to the many available online tools, and not only for the real estate agent but the buyer too.

Prospects are in control of the buying or selling process, more so today than any time prior. This fact is no surprise to real estate professionals, who have found their roles completely redefined in the past several years. Today's home buyers and sellers are leading the encounter. They are educating themselves. In addition, they increasingly turn to sources, other than the profession itself, for information to guide their path to making an informed decision.

The age of the internet has created a positive revolution for buyers, sellers, and real estate professionals that have collapsed the long process into a rather short business practice, whereby all parties do much of the work before the buyer has even visited the area or *Open House.*

Many real estate websites list homes with open houses first when a consumer searches their site. Most real estate websites allow consumers to search by open-house date because they have found that consumers like to search that way.

Realtor.com and others have become a huge real estate source; "Bible", if you will, and its value is its ability to allow profiling for the buyer, rather than most of the other real estate print advertising, which is nothing other than real estate agent imaging. Although there are many interesting internet search sites, Realtor.com commands a leading position and is viewed by 65% of the prospective buyers before they visit the property.

As a real estate agent, it is important that the knowledge of the market is more so together, to better assist the consumers of today. Realizing that in some scenarios, as the real estate agent, it won't be uncommon that the buyer knows more about the property before you even meet them.

BE THE RESIDENTAL PRO!

Some homebuyers I met at one of my open houses. They bought the *Open House*.

Be familiar with the *Open House* and surrounding area. Have an understanding of any pending and "SOLDS", that might have an impact on the *Open House* area.

The buyer might be looking for a different home other than the *Open House* and knowing the surrounding area might provide to be beneficial. I always recommend knowing and having details to at least two other homes for sale close by. It is a great way to open other possibilities to a prospect exploring other options suitable to their needs.

iPad or Tablet to Sign-in Visitors

If you do not have one iPad or Tablet readily available, it would be a good idea to buy one, you may find them inexpensively from under $200. Electronic sign-in helps to eliminate typos and gain correct information of visitors and potential buyers. Many times visitors either have bad penmanship or fail to provide adequate information. Having a tablet eliminates these issues as well as helps to organize visitor contacts for efficient follow-ups and feedback.

Leave without Saying Bye

What is one of the most IMPORTANT reasons why we are doing the *Open House*? To have the opportunity to meet some people "prospects" who might be thinking of buying or selling shortly. Another important reason is also to get contact names, phone numbers or email addresses of who visited the home. And to utilize your home marketing skills to turn those prospects into buyers, or sellers.

Asking the right question and in the right way makes all the difference. I wouldn't suggest a closed-ended question, such as, "Will you sign in my guestbook?", unless gambling is your specialty. In those circumstances, the odds are something close to a 50/50. Or, you could use my personal favorite with a much better chance of success, like…

"WOULD YOU DO ME A FAVOR"? .. *(wait for the answer)* .. "COULD YOU PLEASE SIGN MY GUESTBOOK"?

When asked the question the right way, the typical universal law of response is, "Sure!", "Absolutely" or "No problem."

When you have people that do sign-in on your guestbook, it won't be uncommon to see them fill in just their name and email address, or simply their name. If you do catch it in time before they leave, then just ask for the remaining information such as phone number and email. Make notes of important concerns next to the prospects name on the guestbook, or on a separate notepad to be viewed later.

Now that you have contacts in your guestbook, it's time to follow up with them, so go to work.

What's the point of having an *Open House* if there is no system of follow-up?

These are HOT LEADS! If you do nothing with them, then how can you expect to succeed? Going through the motions of prospecting without follow up is like Bungee jumping off a tall building, except without the Bungee rope. You certainly can't expect a success!

It is suggested to follow up with these potential "prospect", at least 3 times. Thank them for coming to the *Open House*. Ask them if you can notify them of future upcoming *Open Houses*. Stay present in their mind and thought. What does it cost to send an email?

If all you have is an email address left by your *Open House* guest, make sure you do intend to follow up with it. I had a prospect couple that visited one of my open houses, and the email address was all the information I had on that couple. I sent two follow up emails over the course of a week, both with no reply. On my third email attempt, I sent the prospect couple an email message asking had they found their Dream Home yet. I got a RESPONSE!

Looking back, I am certainly glad to have sent that last email, as the husband did reply and, in 30 days' time, not only did I sell them a home, but also listed for sale their current house and sold that, too. It pays to be persistent and to follow up.

Timeline with a Homebuyer

A usual timeline when working with most any prospect once a real estate agent encounters a potential homebuyer with a desire to move forward:

1. Refer homebuyer to mortgage broker and discuss required information for a lender such as job history, credit, etc.

2. Acquire pre-qualification from the mortgage broker with a specified amount as to what a lender will lend to the homebuyer for the purchase.

3. Find a property with the help of the real estate agent that meets the homebuyer's needs, wants, and price range.

4. Make an offer to the seller / listing broker for the property that meets these requirements with the help of the buyer's real estate agent.

5. Negotiate aspects of the contract with the seller / listing broker via the homebuyer's real estate agent until an agreement has been made. When both parties have signed the offer, the property is under contract.

6. Homebuyers to meet with the mortgage broker and begin the loan process.

7. Home inspection on the property.

8. Termite inspection on the property.

9. Shop for homeowner's insurance.

10. Appraisal ordered by the lender.

11. Title insurance ordered by the seller / listing broker through a title company. The title company hired to do this will verify that the ownership is clean on the property and give the buyer insurance in case a problem ever arises at a later time in regards to past ownership.

12. Survey ordered by the lender.

13. Homebuyers to secure home insurance and paid if not through home loan.

14. Proof of insurance provided to the lender.

15. Final approval given for the loan. This is called "Clear to Close" in the real estate industry.

16. Final Walkthrough with homebuyers of the property to ensure all is as it should be.

17. Verification of the HUD-1 Settlement "closing disclosure" Statement. HUD is short for Department of Housing and Urban Development. This is a standard form that the closing agent provides to the seller and buyer at least 24 hours before closing for both parties to verify costs and make any needed changes. It is a statement of how the money involved in the purchase will be exchanged at the closing.

18. Closing (*turnover of ownership from the seller to the buyer*).

19. Utilities changed into the buyer's name.

20. Move in!

LIVE BY THE "GET BY GIVING" PHILOSOPHY. BE A LEADER!

Beautiful home idea for an *Open House*.

ALL ABOUT THE SYSTEMS

There must be a system put in place for everything that is done, from beginning to end, for each *Open House*. A successful *Open House* depends on the right location to attract potential home seekers. This is where studying the area and type of home seekers you desire are key factors. Any home has the potential, but if you're seeking homes to conduct an *Open House* in a price point that you are not comfortable with, then the potential home seeker that comes to visit will suspect that in your conversation.

When planning an *Open House*, remember most home listings a prospect may be searching for are syndicated on the internet by the MLS. The way home listings are syndicated on the Internet makes it simple to market an open house for potential prospects. Put out your open house signs, flags and balloons, and the buyers will come. Hand the prospect who come through the *Open House* a brochure that has substance — beautiful photos, town and school information, and a list of upgrades. Buyers crave information, so give them all you've got. That is what selling is about — sharing all the great reasons for buying what you are offering. You will create a lasting impression about the house and a lasting impression about you as an agent. The potential prospect will love it and they may just buy the house … imagine that!

Many real estate websites list homes with open houses as the first noticeable thing when a consumer searches their site. Most real estate websites allow consumers to search by open-house date, as they have found that consumers like to search that way. Potential prospects love open houses. These prospects are reached by the marketing that is done for an open house, and that is what you are looking for as a listing agent: buyers. The NAR 2013 study also reports that 45 percent of buyers said they used open houses as a source for information in their home search.

Just like when a potential buyer is searching for a home to buy, you as the real estate agent need to search for that right *Open House* that will attract those visitors.

In some areas of the country, those cities will allow you to put directional signs up the night before the *Open House*. Having the right *Open House* signs and placement of those signs for the *Open House* will matter. Be cautious not to place one of your signs on private property or in places they shouldn't be posted, as they could disappear. Or even better, some disgruntled home-owner for whom you place a sign on their property appears at your *Open House*.

The National Association of REALTORS® note that only 8 percent of homes are sold by conducting an *Open House* on the home listing. Personally, I feel those numbers are off. My experience, on the other hand, has been a bit different. Approximately 25 percent of my listings have sold through open houses. Remember, a top notch REALTOR® will conduct an *Open House* at a high level of execution with plenty of buyer leads from the efforts. This includes actively promoting the *Open House* on the

MLS, websites, social media, and Realtor.com, Zillow, and *Open House* signs.

Once at the home, actively market the features and benefits of the home to the home guests as they walk through your active *Open House* (*pointing out the extras that have been added, your favorite things about living in the house and the neighborhood*). Also, knowing the surrounding neighborhood details along with recently sold homes and the active listings in the area will give a buyer confidence in your house, that they will not need to look elsewhere. During this time, at the *Open House,* your houseguest has the opportunity to see you as a true real estate professional, rather than just some salesperson.

Everyone has been to the *Open House* to get a cookie and water, as the REALTOR® sits at the kitchen island and says, "Let me know if you have any questions." This is a prime example of what NOT to do when conducting an *Open House.*

- Find ideal *Open House.*

- Create a plan (When to do it & Why).

- Preparation (Signs, material, vendors & etc.).

- Execute.

- Follow-up .. Follow-up.

- Repeat.

FOR SUCCESS IT ALL ABOUT THE NUMBERS.

Don't forget to follow up with all your *Open House* visitors later by phone or email, this will add value mileage to your real estate career.

Some numbers to consider; if one agent does three more open houses than the other agent, who only does one per month, the latter agent has the potential to be 4 TIMES more successful than the former.

SUCCESS ONLY WORKS IF SYSTEMS & CONSISTENCY ARE APPLIED.

Homebuilders Know

They know their product and how to sell it. A homebuilder usually spends quite a bit of time in the planning and preparation phase of development. That's why most builders first break ground by building a model home. Homebuilders realize the sales activity that will happen at a model home will be somewhere from 85% to 95% due to the imagery and concept of the model home. Both developers and builders know if they build it, the people will come flowing.

Homebuilders are more than happy to invite real estate agents to come and view their new units or projects and encourage them to ask any and all questions they might have. Relationship building is the perfect way to get to know the builders in your area; spending some time getting to know each homebuilder and working styles will help you choose the best builder to work with. Don't overlook the builders; they love it when real estate agents ask to host an *Open House*.

Usually, how many days a week might you find a model home open to the public? If you said 7 days, you're about right. It begs the question, does having a model home open 7 days a week really work, and the answer is YES!

One might ask, how many days a week does the average real estate agent hold an *Open House*? At most, two days, and traditionally on Saturdays or Sundays. It's also worth mentioning, that the mindset within the real estate community is;

conducting an *Open House* produces very little in results.

It's not too common to find a real estate listing agent holding an *Open House* on their own listing personally. You might ask why. It's simple! The listing already knows they will make a commission on the listing side of the transaction. It's their thinking that it's only a matter of time, and that if they don't sell it personally, some other agent will sell the home.

For a real estate agent that currently doesn't have any available home listings, that's why there's no problem in finding plenty of homes perfect for the opportunity to conduct an *Open House* on.

In general, most agents miss the fact that their five other days of possibility because of real estate conventional thinking. In today's society, people generally have days off from work, other than a Saturday or Sunday. For the people who do work, or have other obligations on a Saturday or Sunday do end up missing the *Open House* opportunities of the weekend.

It's important to mention that some years ago, I mentored an agent on the *Art of the Open House*™, and he went on to do work with some homebuilders in conducting open houses on their model homes to help some of the builder reps that were normally there, so they could take a day off. When that real estate agent was at the model home, not only did he have the opportunities in selling a new home, but if a visitor to the model home had a home to sell, he also gained that opportunity, too.

I believe there are many missed opportunities from real estate agents simply overlooking the possibilities with homebuilders.

Think like a Homebuilder when it comes to preparing for an *Open House*, be open to all POSSIBILITIES.

Homebuilders love *Open House.*

HOMES HOMES & MORE HOMES

What's the best property to do an *Open House* on? Easy answer; ALL OF THEM! Over time, I have conducted an *Open House* in beautiful homes, ugly homes, homes in gated communities and homes that didn't even have the utilities on. One thing I kept in mind was the potential of possibility that the public would have an interest in viewing that home.

Any home, including rental homes, has the potential to generate new people to talk with about Real Estate. You may ask, "why rental homes"? Two reasons, one, you may have a planned *Open House* cancel on you, and two, inventory of available homes for sale in your area may be low. Regardless, if you keep in perspective that the property really holds the opportunity for you, the agents, to speak with people about what? REAL ESTATE! What a cool concept.

Nonetheless, choosing the right home is important. Don't be the agent that chooses a home that takes 15 *Open House* signs to navigate to. Your home visitors will get lost trying to find you. Remember planning when choosing a home for an *Open House*. It is ideal to find one that is off or at least close to the main road.

Choose a home that may be no more than 4 to 5 streets in from the main road. Making it easy to find you is vital. That could make the difference between a great turnout and a poor turnout of visitors to the *Open House*. As a real estate agent, considering conducting an *Open House* on a property sometimes, it's wise to visit the home 1st to see if it would be an ideal home.

Doing an *Open House* is explicitly simply a numbers game.

When a real estate agent doesn't have any property listing of their own, then that's NO PROBLEM! Choose another agent's listing and in some cases think outside the box, and choose a listing from another agent from another company. So long as the other agent or broker agree, you're in BUSINESS! Also, homebuilders are a GREAT source.

If you provide feedback on their listing, most listing agents are fine with you doing the *Open House*. Most Listing Agents are happy to have you do an *Open House* on their listing.

Some agents may ask, "Why do you want to do an *Open House* on my listing"? My response was, "It will generate traffic to your listing and maybe, with luck, I might SELL IT"! If it is a competing company's listing, I will use generic *Open House* signs and fliers, so not to take away from the image of their listing.

It is important to understand; YES, it is possible to do an *Open House* on a property listing, that is not within your own company. The key rule is, so long as you have the permission from the listing agent to conduct an *Open House* on their property listing, you are okay. If you intend to conduct an *Open House* on other company property listings, remember to stress to the listing agent your intent to use generic *Open House* signs and fliers, so not to take away from the image of their listing.

Over the years, I have successfully conducted an *Open House* on other company property listings. Yes, on occasion you will find that some of those agents would much prefer to handle their own *Open House*. Fear not, if you are in a real estate area like Dallas/Fort Worth, where there are at least 10,000+ homes for sale in the month. You will no doubt find an *Open House* to conduct from the many available.

If you don't have some custom searches set up on your MLS main page when you log in, this would be a good time to do so. Many agents and especially new real estate agents don't realize how powerful your search tools are in the MLS. You can define a custom search on just about anything. I usually had one main search for homes under the "occupancy." I was able to view either homes that were for sale and occupied or vacant homes. If I needed to hunt for a fast home to do *Open House* on, I might search for vacant homes, then contact the listing agent and ask to do an *Open House* on their listing.

Friday & the House is Gone

Occasionally, you have an *Open House* already prepared and either the sellers' cancel at the last minute, or even better, the listing agent calls to say they've put the property under contract and to cancel the *Open House*. NO PROBLEM! Just as mentioned before: planning is vital, as well as having a backup *Open House* on standby.

In these instants, a vacant home is a GREAT substitute, due to the short notice. I have had great results with both occupied and vacant homes. I usually choose vacant homes for two reasons, one, most agents don't like hosting them, and two, there were no sellers I had to plan around. Sometimes, if you search you may find a vacant home, ones that are staged with furniture are more ideal.

Having contact with other agents and homebuilders will help when a planned *Open House* has been canceled.

REMEMBER, generating leads is all about consistency. No one became SUCCESSFUL without applying it!

ALL HANDS ON DECK

When preparing for an *Open House*, you will find many real estate vendors more than happy to pitch in with your efforts. When possible, build those relationships with vendors who best suit your ideas and vision for the *Open House*. Many of these vendors will be happy to join you, as they too desire to build their business relationships and might have many useful tools to better assist your planning. As you begin to prepare, you will find that some of these vendors will provide snacks and drinks for the *Open House* visitors.

- Title Companies / Escrow Companies.

- Loan Officers.

- Home Inspection Companies.

- Party Planners.

- And many more...

Not all agents agree on the importance of refreshments, but some think they're a good idea. I knew of an agent that would sometimes invite food trucks to his open houses and gave away sports tickets, notebooks or other trinkets. Serving cookies and drinks get the visitors to stop by, interact with the agent and look at the *Open House*.

Open House Slideshow

If you desire to stand out from the other real estate professionals, than consider preparing an *Open House* slide show. Most home sellers these days have a smart TV. In the rear or on the side you'll find a USB port to connect a mobile device. This is the perfect opportunity to create a home slide show highlighting the neighborhood including places to eat, parks, schools, and historical points of interest. It can help to educate potential buyers on the neighborhood, and have them picture themselves at all of the cool places you decide to showcase.

Consider having a couple of exotic car dealers on the list of go to vendors. I once had a local new car dealer drop off a $105,000 Mercedes-Benz S500 for my *Open House*. All vendors want a piece of the action to market their brand, too, and if you put enough thought into the planning of your *Open House*, it may stand-out more than others do.

Mercedes-Benz Dealer delivered a car for my *Open House*.

While we are on the topic of asking vendors to help with your *Open House*, this is a good time for me to bring up RESPA. Just to ensure that you, the *Open House* agent, comply, it is best to review what RESPA has to say if any of the vendors that would want to help, decide to contribute or pay for something. As the real estate agent, you may want to get the latest guidelines and rules regarding what vendors can or can't pay for.

Example: When a title company hosts an agent luncheon at an *Open House*, they are providing food in hopes of meeting agents - just as Real Estate agents hold open houses. One of the questions that may come up, is what the vendor offering for help allowable under RESPA? The answer may be "Yes" and "No". It really depends on what the vendor is offering and if that violates RESPA.

Let's say a real estate agent requests a title company to pay for a lunch that the real estate agent was looking to host, and the title company agrees. The payment from the vendor would be a thing of value for, or in the hopes of, the referral of settlement services in one's business.

If, however, the title company paid for the lunch, but <u>attended</u> the *Open House* and gave a brief presentation, or prominently displayed a sign indicating the title company's name and distributed brochures about the title company during the *Open House*, there is a reasonable argument that this activity is a form of advertising and therefore acceptable and okay. If one is not sure, getting clarification for your real estate broker is always best.

SIGN PSYCHOLOGY

An *Open House* is a legal excuse to plaster the neighborhood with your name. Sign restrictions in most communities would never allow you to post signs all over the area, the exception being *Open House* signs. Some communities also prohibit those and others have tried, so if you can do it, don't be STINGY.

Use *Open House* signs strategically to draw traffic to your *Open House*. Here's how: Use multiple types of signs that are visible and legible from a distance (at least 30 feet), and place directional signs to advertise in a five-block radius to reach a wider public view.

Pass fliers out the day before to the neighbors closest to the *Open House* (10 to 15 homes). That GAINS listing opportunities. A neighbor considering listing their home for sale will stop by to see his neighbors home for ideas.

The success of your *Open House* should not be measured by how many possible buyers you picked up. The success of your *Open House* should be measured according to the number of neighbors you have made a positive impression upon. Think of it as a low key block party; you want the neighbors to stop in.

Just a thought for a moment; can you imagine if a real estate agent was consistent with conducting regular open houses, and how it would look in a short period? The people in the area would begin to have the impression that real estate agent is the dominating force in the community. I remember one specific agent in which that was the case. Come every weekend, you would see his *Open House* signs with his name on them everywhere.

Small Broker Becomes a Big Broker

Let's take this further. Say, you are a real estate broker in a small office. Let's say an office size of 10 to 15 real estate agents in total, and you want to grow your real estate firm. What do you think is the cheapest and effective way to make that possible?

Come the weekend, plaster the town with directional signs at major road intersections and open houses. Maybe a real estate broker with a smaller firm wants to compete in the local area against those bigger offices that have 100 plus agents in their offices. It's simple! Teach your smaller office agents the *Art of the Open House*™, all of the techniques and knowledge it offers.

Begin with the techniques of *Art of the Open House*™, two things will begin to happen; first, one of those 10 or 15 agents will begin to produce for your office via *Open House* consistently. Two, with the community, who will be constantly seeing your office *Open House* signs everywhere, will begin to believe your little real estate firm is a POWERHOUSE real estate company of 100 plus agents.

That is exposure money can't buy, and with any luck, those other agents from other companies will take notice, wondering what makes your real estate firm different than others. Real estate professionals are typically attracted to success and may choose your firm as a viable option to call home.

TOOLS OF THE TRADE

Having some *Open House* signs would be a start. I would recommend two sets. One set of generic, another set with you and your company info on them. Generic set for just in case your *Open House* is for a builder or another company for whom you don't work for.

Generics can be picked up at your local Board of REALTORS® or any Lowes or Home Depot. Custom signs can be made be any local or online printer.

It would be wise to consider some *Open House* directional signs so that they may be put up the night before the *Open House*. Not to mention, save setup time come the day of the *Open House*.

Open House signs, Directional, A-Frames, and Feather Flags should be in your arsenal of tools. Don't forget the guestbook, as that will be the 2nd most important item in that *Open House* arsenal.

Some sample *Open House* signs, A-frame and many more that work GREAT!

To Do List

Things to have or have ready either the day before or the day of the *Open House*. Nothing says you're the true professional better than being prepared for your *Open House*.

- *Open House* signs and directional.

- Guest Registry.

- Details on property (Property sheet, CMA, utility info, property disclosures & etc.).

- Info on 2 to 3 surrounding properties.

- Balloons (if needed).

- Food and/or drinks (if needed).

- Venders (if needed).

When your visitors arrive at your *Open House* now, it's time to amuse, amaze, surprise, and delight them with the information you have prepared for them.

When it comes to food, you can go as fancy as you want to, but hot dogs on the grill, chips, water, soda, and coffee are all you really need. The idea is to slow them down so you can find out who they are and why they are there.

It's important that during the *Open House*, the agent creates a neutral environment. If the home has anything that could be considered the least bit controversial (like an animal head on the wall, or a photo of the seller(s) with a polarizing politico), take it down for the duration.

As the *Open House* agent, it is recommended to go as far as removing anything that is personal (family photos, drawings on the fridge), this gives the feeling of a blank slate, that might help potential buyers picture themselves in the house. I have heard other agents take an opposite view, "People are buying a house, they want to live in it, and they want to know that human beings have lived in it." Either way, close all the toilet lids and get rid of those fuzzy (or carpeted) lid covers.

Also, consider removing area rugs in favor of bare floors. You want potential buyers to see the beautiful floors. It gives them a feeling of space that's not chopped up by the area rugs.

When conducting the *Open House*, very rarely does it work out for the buyers and sellers to meet while the *Open House* is underway. From a practical standpoint, when prospects are walking through an *Open House*, they want some anonymity. With the homeowner(s) there, the prospects can't speak freely. It recommended that during the duration of the *Open House* that the homeowner(s) find other activities outside of the *Open House*.

Tips for a Successful Open House

1. Don't be a chatterbox. Greet your visitors, give them your card and a property brochure, and allow them peace and quiet while they tour the home.

2. Be honest about the home's features and improvements.

3. Don't drop vague hints about offers having been received for the home if that's not the case. When the truth later comes out, the prospect may feel manipulated and back out of the whole transaction.

4. Make copies of presale home and termite inspection reports available to prospective buyers along with estimates of the costs for any needed repairs or fumigation.

5. If your state requires a disclosure, form, have it completed ahead of time, and make copies available to prospective buyers.

6. Display photographs of popular neighborhood amenities (e.g., local parks and recreation center).

7. Have comparable sales data available.

8. Give visitors property information sheets with important facts about the home and the community. Examples include a flyer highlighting the home's features, summaries of room size, lot size, taxes, and assessments; and a map showing the location of schools, hospitals, public transportation, libraries, supermarkets and other services and retailers.

9. Ask visitors for immediate feedback about the home. Also, use a guest book to collect visitors' names, telephone numbers, and e-mail addresses. Follow-up with a phone call or e-mail after the event.

10. Don't forget to turn off the lights, close the drapes, remove the guest book and brochures, and lock up before you leave.

TECHNICALS

These steps are important for having online traffic to the *Open House*. Have the listing agent (if not your listing) set it up on the listed property within the MLS for *Open House* (that way it feeds data to Realtor.com, Zillow, Trulia and any other 3rd party sources). If it is your listing, inform the office or staff to put your *Open House* on the company website and social media accounts.

If needed, advertise and get the word out on social media like Facebook, Instagram, Twitter, LinkedIn and many more. If you don't have a Facebook or other social media, I would recommend doing so. Facebook has a great tool that will allow the user to set up a business page. That is where I recommend setting up a Business Real Estate page. Also, for some free advertising opportunities, join some local groups that will allow you to share updates to coming open houses.

Ideal times for *Open House* on the weekend are Saturdays from 2 pm to 5 pm and Sundays from 1 pm to 4 pm. If choosing *Open House* on the weekdays, the recommended time is from 3 pm to 6 pm.

Most Real Estate agents underestimate how powerful a weekday *Open House* can be. Think about it; there is literally no competition other than the homebuilders who have their model homes open. Homebuilders have visitors to their model homes all throughout the week, not to mention weekends, too. I have found that if one does conduct an *Open House* during the weekday, the ideal timeframe is from 3 pm to 6 pm.

Another brilliant concept is what I call *Open House* Blitz. That is where the *Open House* agent holds two open houses for the day. In those cases, it is ideal to pick two homes within a couple of miles for each other. To effectively work that scenario, you would normally have the 1st *Open House* starting at 10:30 am and end at 1 pm, then have 2nd *Open House* starting at 2 pm and end at 4:30 or 5 pm. To do an *Open House* Blitz, it is usually best on a Saturday or Sunday.

To get a better idea of what your competition is doing, visit other open houses in your surrounding area to get a better idea of any shortcomings that may or may not possessed. When evaluating other open houses, see how those homes are staged and listen to what the *Open House* agent(s) say. Make a note of the features they point out - observe how they are with potential prospects. As you walk through, try to listen to prospect's reactions with the *Open House* agent. In advance, it will give you a good perspective on what to do and not do when at your own *Open House*.

- Greet the *Open House* visitor at the door.

- Welcome and thank them for coming.

- Hand them information on the property.

- As they look at the information, talk about a special feature or two in the home that they may want to notice as they go through the property.

- Ask for their name, phone number, and e-mail address, or have them fill out an *Open House* register so you'll have their contact information.

Like you learned in kindergarten, if you can't say anything nice, don't say anything at all. Again, the seller(s) still call the place home, so don't badmouth it during the *Open House*. They just might have a hidden camera.

FINAL THOUGHTS

Hopefully, the information that has been covered here will bring to light the unlimited possibilities of *Open House*. There are plenty of winning techniques and strategies for acquiring prospects. For me designing a strategy around *Open House* marketing was KEY, it was a revelation and a game-changer for my early career. Since 2003, I have made numerous discoveries to help refine the *Art of the Open House*™ into what it is today.

To help you stay motivated I have compiled some of the best motivating quotes from famous speakers and historical figures:

"Our greatest glory is not in never failing but in rising up every time we fail".

\- Ralph Waldo Emerson

"If you believe in what you are doing, then let nothing hold you up in your work. Much of the best work of the world has been done against seeming impossibilities".

- Dale Carnegie

"There are only two ways to live your life. One is as though nothing is a miracle. The other is as if everything is".

- Albert Einstein

"The nearest way to glory is to strive to be what you wish to be thought to be".

- Socrates

"Go confidently in the direction of your dreams. Live the life you've imagined".

- Henry David Thoreau

"Simplicity is the key to brilliance".

- Bruce Lee

"The world has the habit of making room for the man whose words and actions show that he knows where he is going".

- Napoleon Hill

"The greater danger for most of us is not that our aim is too high and we miss it, but that it is too low and we reach it".

- Michelangelo

"The secret of getting ahead is getting started".

- Mark Twain

"It was character that got us out of bed, commitment that moved us into action, and discipline that enabled us to follow through".

- Zig Ziglar

Keep in mind according to the NAR 2013 Profile of Home Buyers and Sellers, driving through neighborhoods is one of the top buyer activities, and if the house is open, they will stop on in! The NAR 2013 study also reports that 45 percent of buyers said they used open houses as a source for information in their home search. So don't let the naysayers beat you down and try to convince you that doing an *Open House* is a waste of time. These types of people "naysayers" usually have nothing good to say; to them you cannot do anything right by their eyes. Any agent may overcome the negative hurdles in his or her career with the right positive thoughts and creative imagination needed, and jump to a real estate office with the right approaches for his or her success.

BE A RESIDENTIAL PRO!

Closing key things to remember …

- *Open House* is about numbers.

- Planning & preparation of the *Open House.*

- Open-ended Questions for the WIN.

- Meet, Greet and relationship build.

- Be alert for the opportunities & signals of a prospect.

- Don't sell the *Open House* (It will sell to the right person).

- Be a residential PRO.

- Success only works if systems & consistency are applied.

- Get others to assist with you *Open House.*

- Signs, signs & more signs .. Don't be stingy.

Remember, if you currently don't have any properties listed, that shouldn't stop you. You can be out there this week or weekend in an *Open House* connecting with potentially 3 to 6 new prospects.

I know of no other book, pamphlet or training course that will go into the depth with as many key details to help you the real estate agent in understanding the amazing possibilities with *Open House.*

As a real estate professional your future is in your hands, now it's up to you to find success hopefully, a little easier now. To a brighter real estate career, see you at the TOP!

ABOUT THE AUTHOR

When my real estate career began in 2002, I, like so many others, approached it with all the excitement and passion, a can-do attitude. Within eight months, I was all but out of a real estate career until one day when a profound game-changing experience would be revealed, and my real estate career would instantly transform.

Before entering real estate, I was in another profession as I acquired my real estate license in mid-2002. In my prior field of work, I had the honor to be among the top in the insurance industry and thought immediately upon entering the real estate profession I made the naïve assumption I would be an instant SUCCESS. Keep in mind; I was not aware of the actual mechanics of success, let alone in a position to speak about success. At the time, it was an unknown illusion for me. All that was going for me in my favor was an unconscious misunderstanding of the "Burning Desire" to succeed.

Most real estate offices say they are the best in training real estate agents; mine was no different. I was taught how to master writing contracts and listing agreements, how to prospect, send out postcards, prepare mailings, and many more things. With the sense that my real estate trainers were true wizards of real estate knowledge, I was sure to hit it BIG.

Seven months went by after attempting many failed prospecting methods to generate home sales, also while taking into consideration the guidance of my office broker, coaching from various real estate trainers, and words of wisdom from other experienced agents. I HAD NOTHING! Not seeing the BIGGER picture, I still had no direction at what appeared to be a not so promising future in real estate. Now entering the eighth month, I began to discover how wrong those expectations were, I found myself saying, "That was ok, things will change," but they didn't.

As my frustration mounted, the 10th month was nearing with no real sun on the horizon for my real estate career, and stress was settling in. My inner soul searching took over. My thoughts began to ponder, "I may need to seek another career...", (*see a negative thought*) like so many find themselves thinking when things are not working out in business. Nevertheless, I kept telling myself, "I'm a fighter; I will find a way." This was one of my darker moments in life. All I was living on now was, "Hope and Faith," I had nothing else left.

Not too long after, I had a friend who was making it wildly successful in real estate. Still financially stumbling in my career to find my niche, I approached him with reluctance; I contacted him by phone, hoping for that magic pill of success. When I spoke with him, I told him my little short story of how I was, "desperately searching", to find a way to make it in real estate.

Later in that week, I met up with him at an *Open House* he was hosting in Del Mar, California. His name was Kevin, and what he would say to me that day would set me on a path to change my thinking about my real estate career. What Kevin did that day that I unconsciously failed to see, and it wouldn't be until 15 years later that I could see. It had nothing to do with my selling techniques or his skill at training, but it had everything to do with my conscious mind seeing the vision and believing with feeling in my heart the "magic pill" was the way to success.

When saying I attempted everything back in 2002, that would be an understatement. Even as late as writing the book: "*Art of the Open House*"™, I still was no closer to understanding the much-needed revelation behind it all.

The most essential component that I had failed to see during this time was the Mind Power needed to make the difference. Without understanding the power of the subconscious mind, all attempts to grasp hold of success will fade into the sunset. A person's destiny cannot be received if the mind is stuck in the past, learn from the past, live in the present, and create a new future.

The thoughts you think, that you will become.

If you think you are a success, a success you will be.

BOOKS AVAILABLE:

- *Mind Power to Real Estate*

- *El Arte de la Casa Abierta*™ (Spanish Edition)

- *Eyes of a Real Estate Professional*

- *Mobile Home Tycoon*

- *L'arte della Casa Aperta* (Itailan Edition)

www.ingramcontent.com/pod-product-compliance
Lightning Source LLC
Chambersburg PA
CBHW070316240526
45467CB00045B/451